Body Systems:
The
Respiratory
and Circulatory
Systems

BY BARBARA A. DONOVAN

Table of Contents

Introduction 2

CHAPTER 1 Your Respiratory System 4

CHAPTER 2 Your Circulatory System 12

CHAPTER 3 Your Blood 20

Conclusion 28

Glossary 31

Index 32

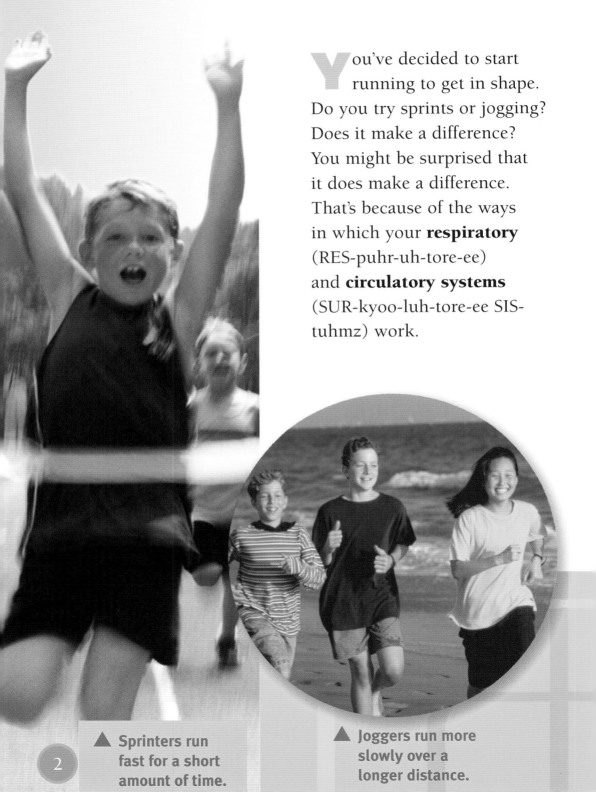

Introduction

You've decided to start running to get in shape. Do you try sprints or jogging? Does it make a difference? You might be surprised that it does make a difference. That's because of the ways in which your **respiratory** (RES-puhr-uh-tore-ee) and **circulatory systems** (SUR-kyoo-luh-tore-ee SIS-tuhmz) work.

▲ Sprinters run fast for a short amount of time.

▲ Joggers run more slowly over a longer distance.

Breathing uses your respiratory system. When you breathe, you inhale, or take in, **oxygen** from the air, and then you exhale, or breathe out, **carbon dioxide** that your body doesn't need. Your heart pumps blood through your circulatory system. By reading this book, you'll learn what these systems are and how they work together. You'll also see how these systems combine to keep you healthy.

▲ Exercise makes you breathe faster and makes your heart pump faster.

Your Respiratory System

Breathe in, and then let that air out. Each breath brings about one pint (about 500 milliliters) of air into your lungs. Take another breath and think about the path the air follows in and out of your body. Which body parts do you use for breathing?

The Parts of the Respiratory System

Nose and Mouth You take in air through your nose or mouth. Doing this warms and moistens the air that you breathe.

Trachea Feel the front of your neck for your trachea. It feels like a long, ribbed tube. The trachea brings air from your nose or mouth into airways, or tubes, in your lungs. Airways split off into smaller branches that end in clusters of tiny air sacs.

1 Solve This

On average, a person breathes 12–15 times per minute while at rest. Count how many breaths you take in a minute. How much air did you breathe in? Answer in pints.

Math ✔ Point
How could estimation help you check your answer?

▲ Yawning, sneezing, and hiccuping all use your respiratory system.

Diaphragm The muscle just below your rib cage is your diaphragm. It relaxes when you breathe out, and it tightens when you breathe in to help you take in more air.

Lungs Take a deep breath and feel your chest puff out. What got bigger were the two lungs in your chest. As you breathe, air flows into your lungs.

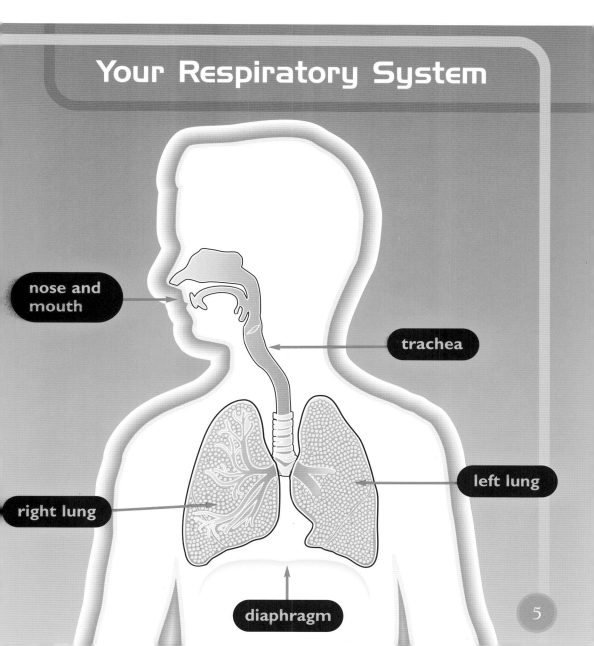

Your Respiratory System

nose and mouth

trachea

left lung

right lung

diaphragm

How the Respiratory System Works

Breathe in and out quickly. Did you breathe out the same air that you just breathed in? No, you breathe in air that contains a colorless and odorless gas called oxygen. You breathe out a gas that your body makes but can't use. This colorless and odorless gas is carbon dioxide. The change from oxygen to carbon dioxide in your cells is a **gas exchange**.

The gas exchange begins when you breathe oxygen into your lungs. Oxygen then moves into blood cells, which travel around your body. Your muscles and organs use oxygen from your blood. They replace the oxygen with carbon dioxide. When the blood returns to your lungs, carbon dioxide enters your lungs and you breathe it out.

▼ This model shows how the trachea splits in your lungs into smaller, tree-like branches, which end in tiny air sacs.

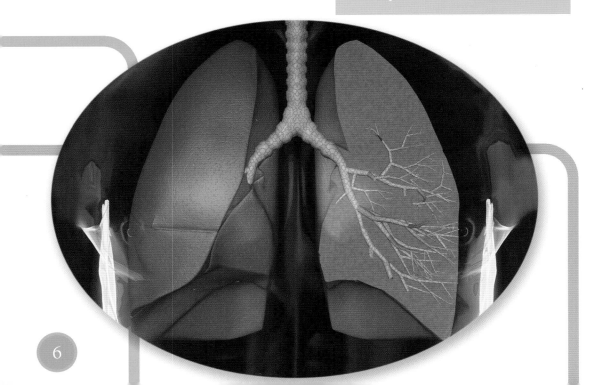

7 Carbon dioxide exits the body through your nose or mouth.

6 Carbon dioxide travels back up your trachea to your nose or mouth.

5 Blood returns to the lungs, your diaphragm relaxes, and you breathe out the carbon dioxide.

4 A muscle or other body part takes oxygen for energy and replaces it with carbon dioxide.

1 Oxygen enters through your nose or mouth as your diaphragm contracts and your chest expands.

2 Oxygen travels down your trachea into your lungs.

3 Oxygen in your lungs transfers into your blood.

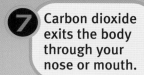

Careers in Science

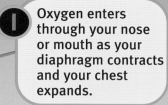

Respiratory Therapist

Some people are born with breathing problems. Others develop breathing problems as they grow older. Respiratory therapists care for those patients. These health care workers work mostly in hospitals. Their job is to check how a patient's lungs are working. Respiratory therapists provide oxygen and medicines to help patients breathe. To have a career as a respiratory therapist, you need two to four years of special medical training.

Exercise and the Respiratory System

Think back to the sprinter and the jogger in the introduction. Both are getting exercise, but the one getting the bigger oxygen boost is the jogger. That's because when you jog, your muscles are working for a longer period of time and you breathe faster. Breathing more often and more deeply pumps extra oxygen into your body. **Aerobic** exercise gives your muscles extra oxygen.

✔ Point

Make Connections

Think about the last time you did an aerobic exercise like jogging. How did the activity make your body feel?

▼ Health experts recommend thirty minutes of vigorous exercise at least three days a week.

Unlike jogging, sprints are **anaerobic**, or exercise without oxygen. When you sprint, your body goes into an oxygen debt. Your muscles use more oxygen than you can breathe in during the short time of a sprint. You gasp for air after a sprint because your body is struggling to "repay" the oxygen that your muscles used up.

2 Solve This

If you follow the advice of health experts and exercise 30 minutes per day, 3 days each week, how many hours of this exercise will you do in a year? Use a calculator if needed. (Hint: 1 year = 52 weeks and 60 minutes = 1 hour)

Math ✓ Point

How can you tell if your answer is reasonable?

◀ A baseball player runs in sprints, or short bursts.

Breathing at High Altitudes

Take a walk in the mountains, and you'll find that at first it's hard to breathe. That's because at higher altitudes there's less oxygen in the air. If you move to a high altitude, eventually your lungs will add blood vessels. These blood vessels will bring you more oxygen so you can breathe more easily.

▲ This mountain climber's lungs have adjusted to working in a high altitude.

Respiratory System Health

Some people are born with conditions, such as asthma, that make breathing difficult. Smoking is another cause of breathing difficulties. Smoking causes the airways in the lungs to close, making it hard to breathe. After a time, the lungs turn from pink and spongy to black and stiff. Here are three tips for keeping your respiratory system healthy.

• Breathe deeply to expand your lungs and take in more oxygen.
• Clean up so dust, mold, and air pollution won't make you sick.
• Don't smoke, and try not to breathe other people's smoke.

Science experiment

Air Pollution

Is the air inside or outside your classroom better for your respiratory health? Each day for a week tape a new index card on the inside and on the outside of a classroom window. Smear each index card with a light coating of petroleum jelly to catch indoor and outdoor air pollution. Use your data to answer the question.

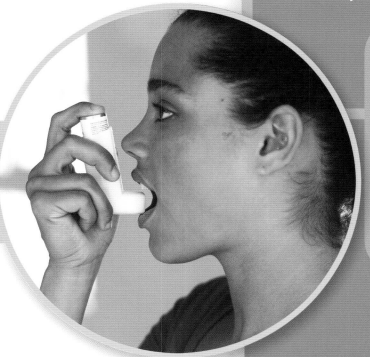

People who ▶ have asthma breathe puffs of medicine from inhalers.

Your Circulatory System

Y ou've probably had a few cuts in your life. When you bleed, you leak a bit of the 10 pints (5 liters) of blood in your circulatory system. In your body, your blood circulates, or travels, in a closed loop. It begins in your heart and travels through blood vessels around your body. It returns through other blood vessels to your heart.

The Parts of the Circulatory System

Heart Your heart is a cone-shaped muscle that pumps blood throughout your body. It's about the same size as your fist.

3

Solve This

About 0.75 of your blood is in your veins. About how many pints is that?

Math ✔ Point

How can you use estimation to check if your answer is reasonable?

blood goes to the lungs from the heart

blood returns to the heart from the body

lower right chamber pumps blood to the lungs

blood goes out to the body

blood returns to the heart from the lungs

lower left chamber pumps blood out into your body

Blood vessels Blood vessels are tubes that carry blood throughout your body. Arteries, veins, and capillaries are three kinds of blood vessels.

Arteries Your arteries are blood vessels that pump oxygen-rich blood out of your heart to all parts of your body.

Capillaries Capillaries are tiny blood vessels that connect your arteries and veins. They deliver oxygen-rich blood to your kidneys, brain, liver, and the rest of your body. Then they send the oxygen-poor blood back to your heart through your veins.

Veins Your veins return oxygen-poor blood to your heart and lungs.

Blood Blood is liquid tissue. It brings oxygen and nutrition to all parts of your body and removes carbon dioxide.

The blood vessels carrying oxygen-rich blood to all the parts of the body are shown in red. These vessels are called arteries.

veins

heart

arteries

capillaries

The blood vessels carrying oxygen-poor blood back to the heart and lungs are shown in blue. These vessels are called veins.

How the Circulatory System Works

Use two fingers to feel the pulse on the inside of your wrist near your thumb. What you feel is the beat of your heart as it pumps blood through your wrist. At rest, most people have a pulse, or heart rate, of about seventy beats per minute. This is your **resting heart rate**.

Solve This

When a doctor or nurse takes your pulse, they often only count the beats for 15 seconds. For the average person at rest, about how many beats would the nurse or doctor count in 15 seconds? (Hint: 60 seconds = 1 minute)

Math ✔ Point

How can you use inverse operations to check your estimate?

▲ The resting heart rate, or pulse, of a well-trained athlete may be as low as forty-five beats per minute.

Your circulatory system begins at your heart (1). It pumps oxygen-rich blood from your lungs (2) into your arteries (3). Arteries pump that blood to your body's major parts such as your brain, liver, and kidneys. Tiny capillaries (4) bring that blood to even your smallest body parts, such as the air sacs in your lungs, and trade it for oxygen-poor blood. Veins (5) return that blood to your heart, which pumps it back to your lungs.

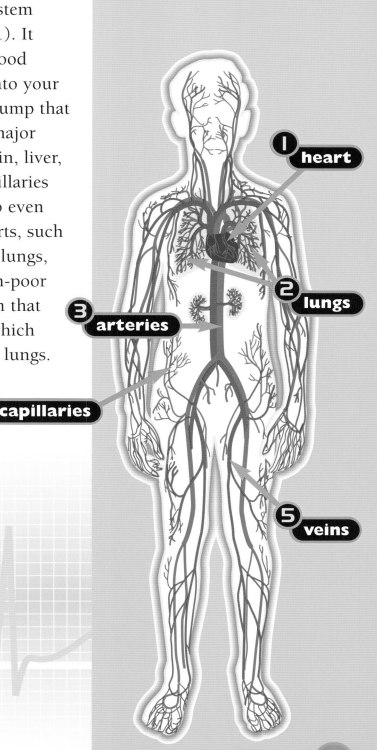

1 heart

2 lungs

3 arteries

4 capillaries

5 veins

Exercise and the Circulatory System

Remember the jogger and the sprinter from the introduction? You learned that your respiratory system delivers more oxygen with an aerobic exercise such as jogging. Aerobic exercise also boosts your circulatory system and makes the chambers of your heart expand. As a result, each beat of your heart pumps more blood to your muscles.

Solve This

How many more milliliters of blood will your heart pump to your muscles in a 30-minute bike ride than in 30 minutes of sitting? Use a calculator if needed.

Math ✔ Point

How can you tell if your answer is reasonable?

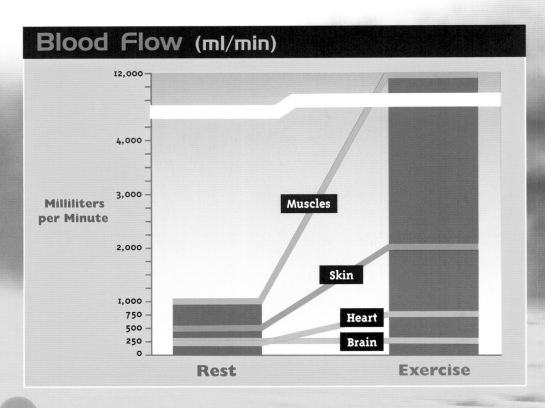

Blood Flow (ml/min)

Milliliters per Minute

12,000

4,000

3,000 — Muscles

2,000

Skin

1,000
750
500 — Heart
250 — Brain
0

Rest   Exercise

As you exercise, extra oxygen-rich blood gets pumped into your muscles. To handle the extra flow, over time your muscles grow more capillaries. Those capillaries now can deliver even more oxygen to your body. All your muscles get healthier—including your heart and the muscles involved in breathing.

✔Point

Think About It

If you wanted to improve the health of your respiratory and circulatory systems, what would you choose to do? Why?

▼ Aerobic exercise not only increases the number of blood vessels in your body, it also increases their size.

A Healthy Heart

If you ever get the chance, ask your doctor to let you listen to your heart. A healthy heart makes a lub-dub sound. Sometimes doctors hear other sounds in your heart. These sounds are called "murmurs." Sometimes murmurs signal problems in a person's heart such as a problem with the heart's valves.

▲ The *lub* part of your heartbeat is the heart resting. The *dub* is your heart pumping blood.

Pioneers in Open-Heart Surgery

1952 Doctor F. John Lewis chills a patient to 81°F (27°C) to temporarily stop the heart and other body functions during the first successful open-heart surgery.

1958 Dr. Åke Senning sews the first pacemaker into a patient's chest to shock the heart into beating regularly.

1967 Dr. Christiaan Barnard completes the first successful heart transplant.

1950

1960

1970

1953 Dr. John H. Gibbon builds and uses a heart-lung machine to circulate blood through the body as the heart is repaired.

Think about a faucet that gets stuck in the open or closed position. Your heart's valves are like that faucet. A valve in a person's heart could get stuck partly open. Then it might flood the arteries with too much blood. A heart valve might also get stuck in the closed position. Then the body can't get the blood it needs. Often doctors can treat these heart problems with medicines, but other heart problems are more serious and need the skills of a surgeon to solve.

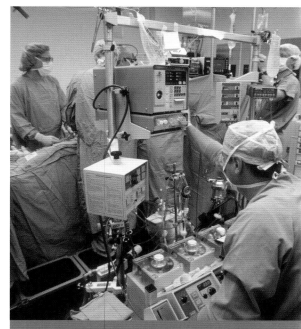

▲ A heart-lung machine circulates a patient's blood while the heart is stopped during open-heart surgery.

1994 Dr. Randas Batista cuts out a damaged part of a person's heart and sews the heart back together.

1980   1990   2000

1982 Dr. William DeVries implants the first artificial heart into a patient.

1998 Dr. Michael DeBakey invents an electric heart.

19

Your Blood

Have you ever wondered why blood from a cut is bright red, but the blood in your veins looks blue? It's related to how your respiratory and circulatory systems work together. Your blood contains different kinds of cells with different purposes. Some cells deliver oxygen and carry away wastes. Others stop bleeding or fight infections.

The Parts of Your Blood

Picture blood oozing from a small cut on your finger. The blood all looks the same, but it's not. Your blood has four parts: plasma, red cells, white cells, and platelets.

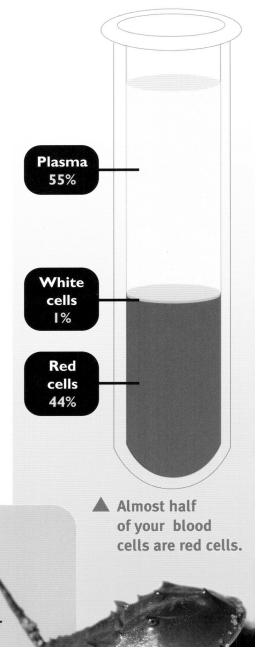

Plasma 55%

White cells 1%

Red cells 44%

▲ Almost half of your blood cells are red cells.

It's a Fact

Blue Blood

A horseshoe crab's blood actually is blue. In human blood, iron makes our blood cells red. The horseshoe crab has copper in its blood. The copper is what makes its blood blue.

Plasma Plasma is the clear liquid part of your blood. It's about 90% water to keep your body's tissues moist. The rest contains dissolved solids such as salt and calcium.

Red cells Red cells carry oxygen from your lungs to your body's tissues. Red cells are about 3 millionths of an inch (8 micrometers) in diameter. Their life span is about 120 days.

White cells White cells fight infections. They're about twice the size of red cells and have a life span of about one year.

Platelets Platelets are bits of blood cells that clump together to stop bleeding.

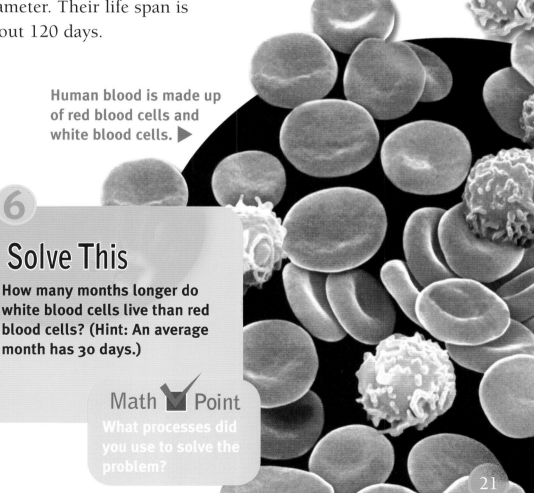

Human blood is made up of red blood cells and white blood cells. ▶

6

Solve This

How many months longer do white blood cells live than red blood cells? (Hint: An average month has 30 days.)

Math ☑ Point
What processes did you use to solve the problem?

Capillaries cover ▶
the grape-like air
sacs in the lungs.

How Your Blood Works

When you breathe in, oxygen travels into your lungs'
air sacs. Capillaries surrounding the air sacs are filled
with oxygen-poor blood. As the air sacs fill with the
oxygen you breathe in, a gas exchange occurs. In less
than a second, oxygen from the air sacs goes into the
capillaries and makes the blood oxygen-rich. At the
same time, carbon dioxide from the oxygen-poor blood
goes into the air sacs. You breathe that carbon dioxide
back into the air around you.

Oxygen from the lungs turns blood bright red. Your heart pumps that oxygen-rich blood through your arteries. In your tissues, capillaries trade oxygen for carbon dioxide. This gas exchange makes the cells a dark, purplish red. The oxygen-poor blood cells move along veins back to the heart and lungs. You breathe out carbon dioxide as blood cells return to your lungs for more oxygen.

They Made a Difference

Leonardo da Vinci was a great painter. But he was also curious about how the human body worked. During his lifetime, medicine was mostly guesswork. In order to learn about the human body, da Vinci examined the heart and other muscles of dead bodies. He filled thirteen sketchbooks with his observations and theories about how body systems worked.

If oxygen makes blood from a cut look red, why does blood in your veins look blue? The answer lies in the thickness of blood vessel walls. Arteries need strong, thick walls because the heart pumps blood through them at great pressure. There's not much pressure on your veins, so their walls are really thin. That's why the purplish blood flowing through your veins looks blue through your skin.

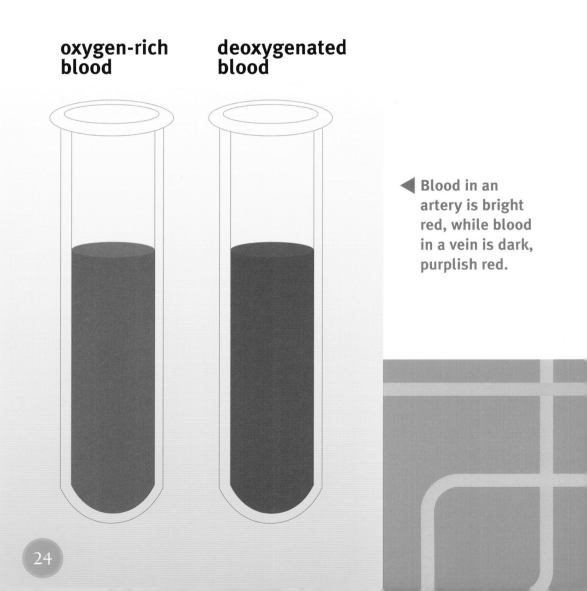

oxygen-rich blood

deoxygenated blood

◀ Blood in an artery is bright red, while blood in a vein is dark, purplish red.

Blood from Your Bones

Did you know that blood is made in your bones? Red cells are made in **bone marrow**, a spongy red substance inside your bones. Your bone marrow is constantly making red cells. One tiny drop of your blood contains more than 5 million red cells. Every second about 3 million red cells die, and your bone marrow makes about 3 million new ones to take their place.

7

Solve This

About how long does it take for your body to make a billion red blood cells? Use a calculator if needed.

Math ✓ Point

How can you use a place-value chart to help you estimate?

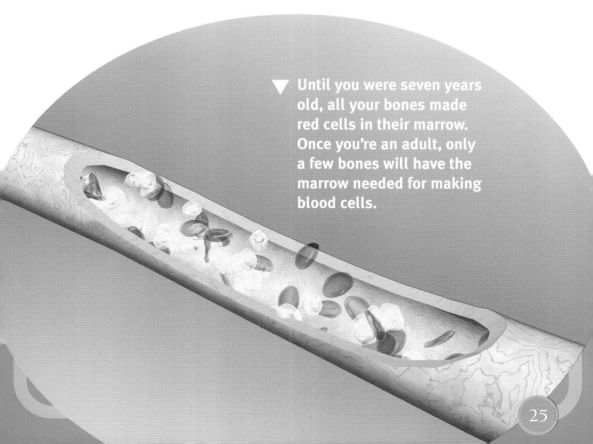

▼ Until you were seven years old, all your bones made red cells in their marrow. Once you're an adult, only a few bones will have the marrow needed for making blood cells.

25

Blood and Your Health

Not everyone is born with healthy blood. Some people are born with blood problems. For example, some kids have to be careful of the slightest bump. Their bodies can't stop bleeding once it starts. For them, a bruise or cut can be very dangerous. This blood disease is called hemophilia (hee-muh-FIL-ee-uh).

everyday science

Scabs

When you get a cut, your body tries to plug the hole by itself. Here's how it does it. First, the broken blood vessel gets smaller to slow the flow of blood. Then, platelets group together in a bunch called a clot. As the clot hardens in the air, a scab forms over the cut to prevent more bleeding and to keep out germs.

Another blood disease is sickle cell anemia (uh-NEE-mee-uh). If you're African American, you have a 1 in 500 chance of having this disease. Red cells usually have an oval shape. Sickle cell anemia causes red cells to have a curved shape. Because of their shape, the cells get caught on each other, clump in veins and arteries, and can cause a lot of pain.

8

Solve This

Approximately 36,000,000 African Americans live in the United States. Of that number, about how many would you expect to have sickle cell anemia? Use a calculator if needed.

Math  Point

Is your answer reasonable? How can you tell?

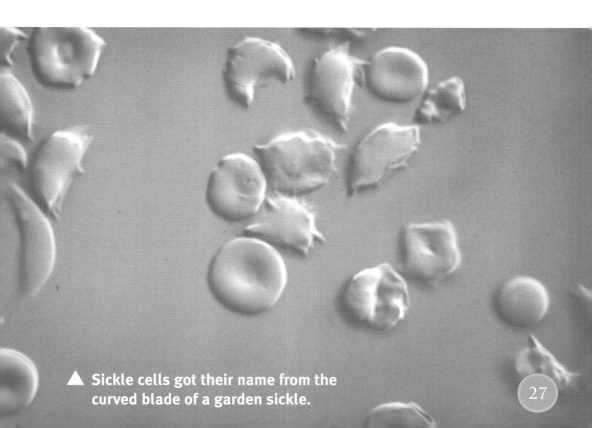

▲ Sickle cells got their name from the curved blade of a garden sickle.

Conclusion

Every minute of every day, you breathe in and out. Your heart pumps blood around your body. Your bones make new blood cells as old ones die. Together your respiratory and circulatory systems keep you alive. How can you keep those systems in top shape? Remember to exercise and eat right, so your body systems will work well for a long, long time.

▼ Keeping in shape keeps your respiratory and circulatory systems in shape, too.

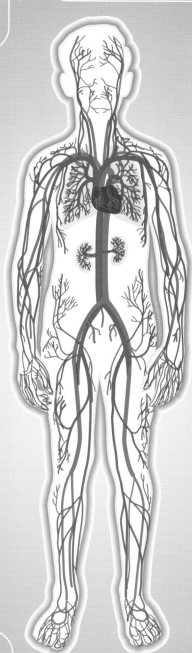

1 Oxygen enters your body as your diaphragm tightens and you breathe in.

2 Oxygen travels down your trachea to your lungs.

3 Oxygen enters your lungs and is transferred to capillaries.

4 Oxygen-rich blood flows from your lungs to your heart.

5 Your heart pumps oxygen-rich blood out your arteries.

6 Your arteries bring oxygen-rich blood to your capillaries.

7 Your capillaries deliver oxygen to your tissues.

8 Your tissues transfer carbon dioxide to your capillaries.

9 Your capillaries bring oxygen-poor blood to your veins.

10 Your veins bring oxygen-poor blood to your heart.

11 Your heart pumps oxygen-poor blood into your lungs.

12 Capillaries transfer carbon dioxide into your lungs.

13 Your diaphragm relaxes and carbon dioxide travels up your trachea to your nose or mouth.

14 Carbon dioxide exits your body as you breathe out.

Solve This Answers

1 Page 4: **Answers will vary. Possible answer: About 9–15 pints**

Math Checkpoint: **You breathe in about 1 pint of air per breath. If you take 12 breaths per minute, you'll take in about 12 pints of air.**

2 Page 9: **78 hours**

Math Checkpoint: **At 30 minutes, 3 times per week, you'll spend 90 minutes, or 1 1/2 hours, exercising each week. That's more than 1 hour per week or 52 hours per year, and less than 2 hours per week or 104 hours per year. 78 hours per year is in the middle between 52 and 104, so the answer is reasonable.**

3 Page 12: **7.5 pints**

Math Checkpoint: **Divide: 7.5 / 10 = 0.75**

4 Page 14: **About 18 beats**

Math Checkpoint: **Divide. 70 / 60 = 1.17. Then Multiply: 1.17 × 15 = 17.55.**

5 Page 16: **330,000 ml**

Math Checkpoint: **The difference in blood flow between bike riding and being at rest is about 10,000 ml per minute. 10,000 × 30 = 300,000. 300,000 is close to 330,000, so the answer is reasonable.**

6 Page 21: **8 months longer**

Math Checkpoint: **Division and subtraction: 120 / 30 = 4; 12 − 4 = 8**

7 Page 25: **About 300 seconds**

Math Checkpoint: **If you line up 1,000,000,000 and 3,000,000, in a place value chart, you can see that you're really comparing 1,000 to 3, so you can estimate 1,000 / 3 to find the answer. 1,000 / 3 is near to 900 / 3, which equals 300.**

8 Page 27: **72,000 people**

Math Checkpoint: **Yes, if you multiply 72,000 by 500, you get back the population of 36,000,000.**

Glossary

aerobic
(ay-ROH-bik) happening in the presence of oxygen (page 8)

anaerobic
(an-uh-ROH-bik) happening without the presence of oxygen (page 9)

bone marrow
(BOHN MAR-oh) spongy tissue inside bones that makes blood cells (page 25)

carbon dioxide
(KAR-buhn digh-OK-sighd) a colorless and odorless gas that is a waste product of cells (page 3)

circulatory system
(SUR-kyoo-luh-tore-ee SIS-tuhm) the heart and blood vessels that move blood in a loop throughout the body (page 2)

gas exchange
(GAS eks-CHAYNJ) the transfer of oxygen for waste carbon dioxide in human blood cells (page 6)

oxygen
(OK-si-juhn) a colorless and odorless gas that is required for human respiration (page 3)

respiratory system
(RES-puhr-uh-tore-ee SIS-tuhm) in humans, the nose, mouth, trachea, lungs, and other organs involved in breathing and carrying oxygen throughout the body (page 2)

resting heart rate
(REST-ing HART RAYT) the number of times per minute that a person's heart beats while at rest (page 14)

Index

aerobic, 8, 16–17

air pollution, 11

air sacs, 4, 22

altitude, 10

anaerobic, 9

artery, 12–13, 15, 23, 29

asthma, 11

blood, 3, 7, 12, 20–27

blood color, 20, 23–24, 28

blood disease, 26–27

blood vessel, 13, 16, 26

bone marrow, 25

capillary, 13, 15, 22–23, 29

carbon dioxide, 3, 6–7, 23, 29

chamber, 12

circulatory system, 3, 12–19, 20, 22, 28

clot, 26

da Vinci, Leonardo, 23

diaphragm, 5, 7, 29

exercise, 3, 8–9, 16–17, 28

gas exchange, 6, 23

health, 3, 16

heart, 3, 12, 15, 18, 23, 28–29

heart-lung machine, 19

horseshoe crab, 20

lungs, 4–7, 10–12, 15, 22–23, 29

mouth, 4, 7

murmur, 18

muscle, 7–8, 12, 16

nose, 4, 7

oxygen, 3, 6–11, 16, 20, 22–24, 29

plasma, 20–21

platelet, 21, 26

pulse, 14

red cells, 20–21, 25–26

respiratory system, 3–11, 16, 20, 22, 28

respiratory therapist, 7

resting heart rate, 14

trachea, 4, 7, 29

valve, 12, 18–19

vein, 12–13, 15, 23–24, 29